The Library
of the
PILGRIMS

William Bradford and Plymouth:
A Colony Grows

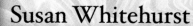

Susan Whitehurst

The Rosen Publishing Group's
PowerKids Press™
New York

To Adam, the artist

Published in 2002 by The Rosen Publishing Group, Inc.
29 East 21st Street, New York, NY 10010

First Edition

Book Design: Maria E. Melendez
Project Editor: Frances E. Ruffin

Photo Credits: Cover and title page (the Pilgrims signing the Compact), pp. 5, 18 © The Granger Collection; cover and title page (settlement of Pilgrims at Plymouth, Massachusetts, 1620), pp. 4, 11, 15, 16, 17, 19 © North Wind Pictures; cover, title page, and p. 12 (the *Mayflower* ship) © Burstein Collection/CORBIS; p. 7 © CHRISTIE'S Images; pp. 8, 10, 22 © Rose Beddington; p. 9 © The Art Archive; p. 20 © Mary Evans Picture Library.

Whitehurst, Susan.
William Bradford and Plymouth : a colony grows / Susan Whitehurst.
    p. cm. — (The library of the Pilgrims)
Includes bibliographical references and index.
ISBN 0-8239-5808-6 (lib. bdg.)
1. Bradford, William, 1588–1657—Juvenile literature. 2. Pilgrims (New Plymouth Colony)—Biography—Juvenile literature.
3. Massachusetts—History—New Plymouth, 1620–1691—Juvenile literature. 4. Governors—Massachusetts—Biography—Juvenile literature.
5. Plymouth (Mass.)—History—Juvenile literature. 6. Bradford, William, 1588–1657. [1. Governors. 2. Pilgrims (New Plymouth Colony)
3. Massachusetts—History—New Plymouth, 1620-1691.] I. Title.
F68.B78 W48 2002
974.4'02'092—dc21

2001000247

Manufactured in the United States of America

Contents

Father of the Pilgrims

William Bradford was not the first **governor** of the Plymouth **Colony**, which later became part of Massachusetts. The first governor was John Carver. When John Carver died in April 1621, William Bradford was elected to be the second governor. Bradford was so loved and respected by the Pilgrims in Plymouth that he was elected governor 30 times! Except for five years when he asked to take a break, he served as governor from 1621 until his death in 1657. Through William Bradford's wisdom and leadership, the Pilgrims survived many difficulties during their first years at Plymouth.

This is a drawing of William Bradford and the Pilgrims celebrating Christmas at Plymouth Colony in 1621.

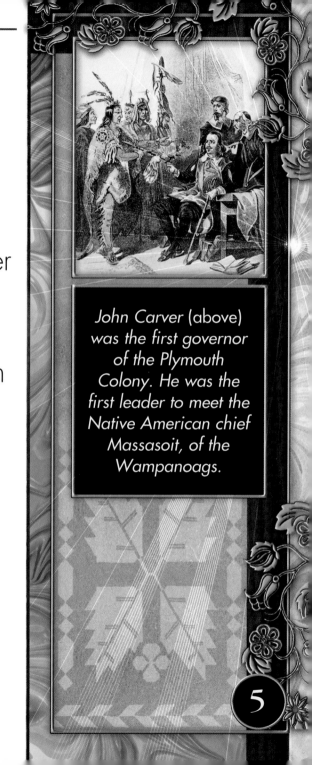

John Carver (above) was the first governor of the Plymouth Colony. He was the first leader to meet the Native American chief Massasoit, of the Wampanoags.

William, the Child

William Bradford was born in the small farm village of Austerfield, England, in March 1590. His family owned several farms in Austerfield and raised sheep. When William was 16 months old, his father died. Although his mother married again, William was raised by a grandfather and later by two uncles. He might have grown up to be a farmer like members of his family if he hadn't become sick. He was an **invalid** for several years. To pass the time, William learned to read and write. There were no schools in Austerfield, so he probably studied with the village preacher.

Only a few chairs were carried to America on the Mayflower. These carved oak armchairs were made in the 1600s.

Religious Questions

The more that William Bradford read, the more he began to question the **religious** laws of England. The Church of England was run by Queen Elizabeth I and later by King James I. It was the law that everyone went to the Church of England. People who did not could be put in prison. William didn't agree with everything taught by the Church of England. As a boy, he met people who were called **Separatists** and who were led by William Brewster. They wanted to **reform** the Church of England. Bradford traveled to Scrooby Manor, 8 miles (13 km), from his home, to hear a Separatist preacher.

◀ *When it became too dangerous to meet at the church, 40 or 50 Separatists began to meet secretly at Scrooby Manor, their leader William Brewster's home.*

King James I, ruler of England from 1603 to 1625, headed the Church of England.

Home on Stink Alley

The Separatists at Scrooby Manor knew they couldn't stay in England. By choosing their own religion, they risked going to jail. In 1607, the Separatists decided to move to Holland where they could practice their religion freely. But first they had to escape from England. William Bradford, who was only 17, tried three times to go to Holland. The first two times, he and the other Separatists were arrested. They finally arrived in Leiden, Holland, in August 1608. William lived with the Brewsters, a Separatist family, in a house on a dark alley called *Stinksteeg*, or Stink Alley.

Bradford once attended church at the Scrooby Parish in Nottinghamshire, England.

When they arrived in Holland, Bradford and the Separatists didn't speak Dutch, the language spoken in Holland. They had to take the lowest-paying jobs.

The *Mayflower* and the Pilgrims

William Bradford stayed in Holland for 12 years. He learned to speak Dutch. When he became an adult, he **inherited** his father's lands in England, which he immediately sold. He used that money to buy a little house and start his own weaving business. In 1612, he married Dorothy May, and in 1615, their son John was born. They might have stayed in Holland, but it was hard for the Separatists to make a living there. They also were worried that their children were becoming more Dutch than English.

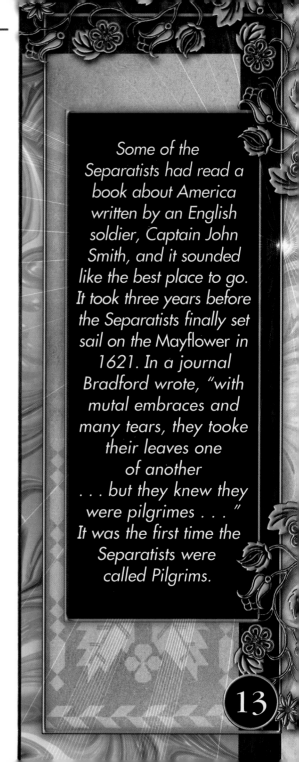

This is a picture of the Mayflower, the ship that brought the Pilgrims to America.

Some of the Separatists had read a book about America written by an English soldier, Captain John Smith, and it sounded like the best place to go. It took three years before the Separatists finally set sail on the Mayflower in 1621. In a journal Bradford wrote, "with mutal embraces and many tears, they tooke their leaves one of another . . . but they knew they were pilgrimes . . ." It was the first time the Separatists were called Pilgrims.

13

Landing in America

After 66 long, terrible days at sea, the *Mayflower*, carrying 102 Pilgrims, sailed into Cape Cod. Before they went ashore, all of the men on the ship signed the Mayflower Compact. This was an agreement that said everyone was equal and that all of the decisions about the colony would be made as a group. It was the beginnings of **democracy** in America. For six weeks, the *Mayflower* stayed in Cape Cod Bay, while Captain Myles Standish, William Bradford, and the other men looked for a good place to settle. Plymouth seemed perfect. It had a hill, a river, and a nice harbor.

During their first winter in Plymouth, nearly half of the Pilgrims died of hunger, illness, and the bitter cold weather.

Shortly after the Pilgrims' arrival in Cape Cod, Dorothy Bradford fell overboard and drowned. There was little time for Bradford to mourn her death. The Pilgrims were in the middle of their hardest winter.

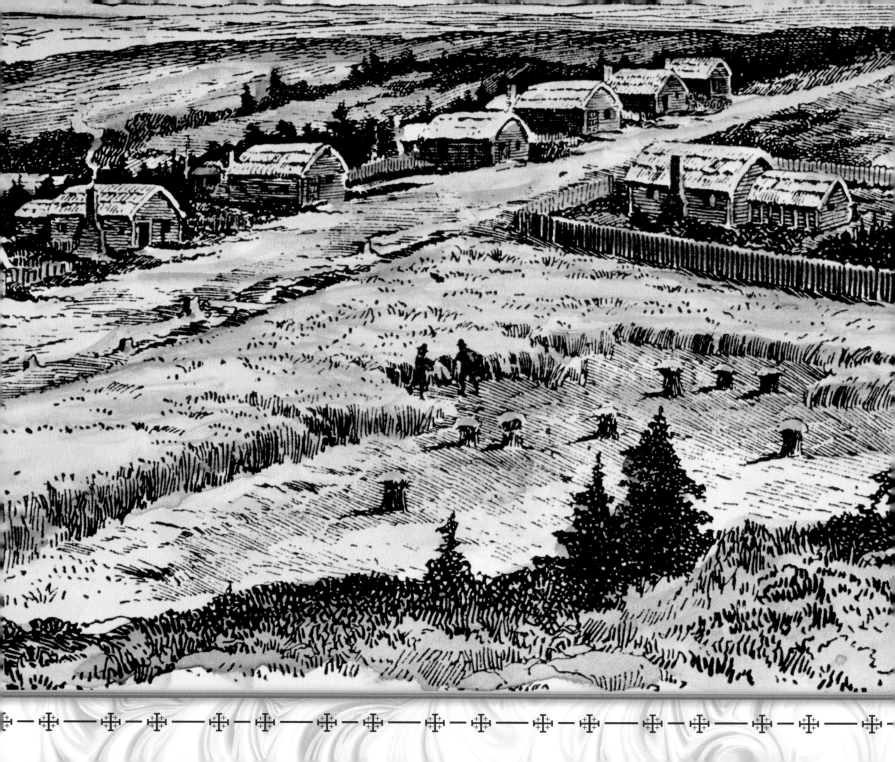

A Growing Colony

The spring and summer brought warm weather, good crops, and the friendship of the **Wampanoag** Indians. It also brought the death of the Pilgrims' first governor, John Carver. The Pilgrims asked William Bradford, then 31, to be the next governor.

Bradford was responsible for giving out **plots** of land in Plymouth for homes. The colony was growing. During the first winter, only one building, called the common house, was built. It was used as a storehouse and as a hospital for sick people. By October, seven one-room houses had been built.

This is a view of the Pilgrims' colony in Plymouth, as it looked in 1622.

The first houses in Plymouth were made of wooden planks and had roofs of straw. People cooked, ate, worked, and slept in one room. By 1624, Plymouth had 32 houses, 180 people, some goats, cattle, pigs, sheep, and chickens. There was also a fort, a storehouse, a wharf, and a graveyard.

17

Squanto (above), a Native American, helped the Pilgrims. Not all Native Americans were friendly. A Naragansett warrior once marched into Plymouth and threatened war by throwing down a bunch of arrows tied with a snakeskin. Bradford filled the snakeskin with bullets and returned it to the Naragansetts. They decided not to attack the Pilgrim colony.

Judge, Peacekeeper, and Businessman

As governor, William Bradford was also the judge for Plymouth. The Pilgrims had laws and everybody had to obey them. It was a crime to steal or to get drunk. Everyone had to go to church on Sunday, and everyone took turns guarding the colony. Bradford also dealt with the Merchant Adventurers. These were businessmen who had lent the Pilgrims money to start their colony, in exchange for which the Pilgrims were to send animal furs back to England. Bradford also worked to keep peace between the Pilgrims and the Wampanoags, Native Americans who lived nearby.

The Pilgrims at Plymouth signed a peace agreement ▶
with the Wampanoag chief, Massasoit, in 1621.

Always Another Chore

Plymouth was a very busy place. Everyone had to work hard to have food and a place to live. There were always chores such as cooking, farming, chopping wood, fishing, and hunting to be done. Everyone had a large vegetable garden by their house. There were **craftsmen** among those who lived in the colony, such as carpenters and **blacksmiths**. One of the busiest homes was the governor's house. William Bradford married again in 1623. His new wife, Alice, had two children of her own. Young John Bradford was brought from Holland to live with the new family.

◀ *Shoemakers were among the craftsmen at the Plymouth settlement.*

William Bradford and Alice had three more children of their own, and they raised some children who had become orphans. So many Pilgrims had died during the first winter that many children were left without parents.

21

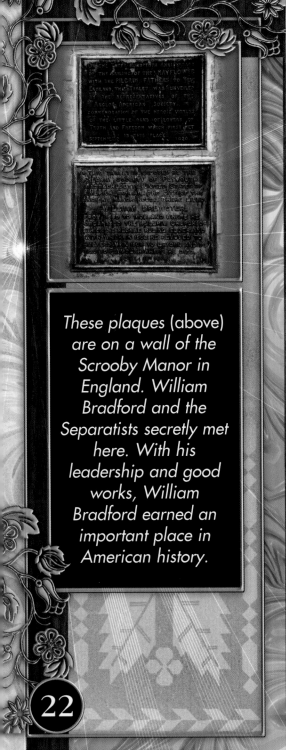

These plaques (above) are on a wall of the Scrooby Manor in England. William Bradford and the Separatists secretly met here. With his leadership and good works, William Bradford earned an important place in American history.

Bradford's Gifts

Most of what we know about Plymouth is based on William Bradford's handwritten book, *Of Plymouth Plantation*. He kept a journal about the daily lives of the Pilgrims. He didn't think the journal was important. He called it his "scribbled writing." It turned out to be the most important source of information about the Pilgrims. His 270-page book was sent to Boston's Old South Church Library. In 1760, it disappeared. Ninety years later, in 1850, it turned up in London. It wasn't returned to Boston until 1897. Like Bradford, his book traveled a lot. When William Bradford died in 1657, the Pilgrims mourned losing the Father of Plymouth.

Glossary

blacksmiths (BLAK-smiths) People who work with metals such as iron to create tools and other metal objects.

colony (KAH-luh-nee) An area in a new country where a large group of people move.

craftsmen (KRAFTS-min) Skilled and creative workers.

democracy (di-MAH-kruh-see) A government that is run by the people who live under it.

governor (GUH-vin-ur) The head of a colony.

inherited (in-HER-iht-ed) To have received something after the former owner dies.

invalid (IN-vuh-lihd) A person who is sick or disabled.

plots (PLOTS) Small areas of ground.

religious (rih-LIH-jus) Faithful to a religion and its beliefs.

reform (rih-FORM) To change or improve.

Separatists (SEH-puh-ruh-tists) A religious group that wanted to separate from the Church of England.

Wampanoag (wahm-puh-NOH-ag) A group of Native Americans who lived in the New England area.

Index

Web Sites

To learn more about William Bradford and the Pilgrims, check out these Web sites:
www.pilgrimhall.org
www.Plymouth-1620.com